Faith

A thought for each day of the year

Philip M. Hudson

Copyright 2019 by Philip M. Hudson.

Published 2019.

Printed in the United States of America.

All rights reserved.

No portion of this book may be reproduced, stored in a retrieval system, or transmitted in any form or by any means – electronic, mechanical, photocopy, recording, scanning, or other – except for brief quotations in critical reviews or articles, without the prior written permission of the author.

ISBN 978-1-950647-21-7

Illustrations – Google Images.

This book may be ordered from online bookstores.

Publishing Services by BookCrafters
Parker, Colorado.
www.bookcrafters.net

Table of Contents

Acknowledgements..i
Preface..v
Introduction..vii

A Thought For Each Day Of The Year...1
About The Author...367
By The Author...369
What More Can I Say?..373

Nephi clearly taught that "it is by grace that we are saved, after all we can do." (2 Nephi 25:23). Latter day Saints, however, sometimes emphasize works to the point that it may seem to others that their faith in the grace of God takes a back seat to their own efforts to earn salvation.

Acknowledgements

In this volume, I have attributed quotations to original authors whenever possible, as well as when I have editorialized their ideas. In many cases, however, my language will naturally reflect the teachings of leaders and members of The Church of Jesus Christ of Latter-day Saints.

The list of those who have contributed to this book is endless. As I have organized my own thoughts, I have realized how heavily I have borrowed from the towering examples of those who, over the years, have been my mystical mentors, my sensible chaperones, my spiritual guides, my surrogate saviors, my compassionate critics, and everything in between.

They are my avatars, manifestations of deity in bodily forms, my na'vi, the visionaries, who communicate with God on a level to which I can only aspire, and my tsaddik, whom I esteem as intuitive interpreters of biblical law and scripture. They are my divine teachers incarnate. They have offered listening ears, extended open arms. lifted my spirits, shown me the way, stretched my mind, reinforced my faith, strengthened my testimony, helped me to discover my wings, given immaterial support, provided of their means, emboldened me with words of encouragement, cheered me on with wise counsel, taught me humility, been there to steady me, soothed my troubled soul, stepped in to nurture me, led me to fountains of living water, wet my parched lips with inspired counsel, and bound up my wounds.

When I think of the influence of a multitude of angels thinly disguised as my family, friends, and peers, I remember the words of Sir Isaac Newton, who, when pressed to reveal the great secret behind his accomplishments, simply replied: "I stood on the shoulders of giants." Of course, at the end of the day, I alone am responsible for the content of this volume. But I hope my interpretations of principles and doctrine will cultivate your interest to dig deeper into the themes woven into this tapestry, by turning to the scriptures and seeking inspiration from the Spirit. My only goal is to help you to expand your insights into the telestial mile markers, the terrestrial truths, and the celestial guidelines that accompany each of us during our quest for enlightenment through faith.

The elements
of God's Plan speak
to our spirits, for every
Gospel principle carries within
itself a witness that it is true. Its
language is universal, and when our
minds have been illuminated by faith,
we enjoy fluency, familiarity, and an
easy comfort with the revealed word
of God that opens up vistas of
eternal proportion before
our eyes.

It is faith that
captures the heart of a little
child before it has been exposed to
the cankering influence and corrosive
elements of the world, before their hearts
are set upon temporal things, and their
spirituality has been so weakened that
the things of God are no longer part
of their daily experience. Better than
the rest of us, little children have a
capacity to "lay aside the things
of this world, and seek for
the things of a better."
(D&C 25:10).

Preface

I love to learn by reading the scriptures, and I often think of St. Hilary, who wrote in the third century: "Scripture consists not in what we read, but in what we understand." In each of the musings within this volume, I have consistently tried to find a scriptural foundation and a spiritual confirmation as I put my pen to paper.

I am continually reminded of Nephi's counsel to press forward with complete dedication and steadfastness, or confidence with a firm determination in Christ, having a perfect brightness of hope, or perfect faith, and charity, or a love of God and of all men. If we do this, feasting upon the word of Christ, or receiving strength and nourishment as we ponder the doctrines of the kingdom, and particularly the principle of repentance, and as we then endure to the end in righteousness, we shall have eternal life, which is the greatest of God's gifts. (See 2 Nephi 31:20).

It is with love, then, that I extend to you the invitation to enjoy this omnibus of random thoughts. Embrace it at face value, and use its exhortations to greater faith as a springboard to your own personal plateaus of discovery, as you are taught by the Spirit to move in the direction of your dreams.

The generation
of our faith follows
an established pattern.
We remember the words of
Jeremiah, who counseled us:
"Ask for the old paths, where is
the good way, and walk therein,
and ye shall find rest for your
souls." (Jeremiah 6:16).

Introduction

If they are fortunate, novice quilters quickly learn a bit of wisdom from the Amish, who make some of the finest quilts in the world. On purpose, the Amish build mistakes into their projects, because they believe that any attempt on their part to design and produce a flawless creation would be a mockery of God, Who alone is perfect. The humility of the Amish makes me think of my own weak attempts to put the thoughts expressed in this omnibus to paper. In His infinite wisdom, God knows very well that I do not need to consciously plan on lacing my efforts with errors. That will come quite naturally, without the need for me to intentionally contribute to my short-comings.

Perhaps this serendipitous collection of musings will do little more than help to define quirks in my personality. Each of us is different, and many things, including our family and friends, the circumstances in which we find ourselves, the quality of our education, and our own personalities, inspire and mold our oral and written expressions. I would like to think that, in this text, all of these influences have been encouraging, affirmative, and constructive.

The reflections within this tome leave the door ajar for the reader, to allow shafts of the light of understanding to creep in. If, as I have expressed my thoughts, I mis-stated myself a few times, or flat-out got it wrong, I ask the patient indulgence and gentle correction of the reader.

Too often, I realize that my communications can be "carefully disguised with hypocrisy and glittering words," as Einstein put it. Although I do fancy myself a wordsmith, I have tried to avoid pedestrian expressions, idle language, and lazy scholarship. I do not pretend to be an authority on the principle of faith, inasmuch as I believe that we are all works in progress, but if you find the factual tone of a particular musing disengaging, the truth is that I typically experienced a deep personal involvement in my interpretation of the principles that illuminated its meaning.

In any event, when you open this volume, I hope you ponder these minute musings with as much enjoyment as I have experienced while creating them.

In matters of faith,
it is not the Lord, but we, who
are on trial. At the Bar of Justice, He
will simply weigh the facts. Our previous
acceptance or rejection of the Gospel will
determine our reward or our punishment.
Trial proceedings have already been
docketed to immediately follow
our mortal experience, and
they will be even-handed
and eminently
fair.

How many times have we read about, or even witnessed, cultural collapse because a faithless society has decayed from within? In every case, iniquity follows those who yield themselves "unto the power of Satan." (3 Nephi 7:5). People do not seem to be able to understand that Lucifer was a first-grade dropout whose influence was the companion of anarchy because it denied the faith and demeaned the intelligent application of knowledge.

When, by faith, we are infused with the knowledge of God, our "bodies shall be filled with light, and there shall be no darkness in (us); and that body which is filled with light comprehendeth all things." (D&C 88:67).

As the white-hot spark of faith, struck off the Divine Anvil of God, ignites the flame of our resolve, we develop the "power to do whatsoever thing is expedient," or right to do under the circumstances. (Moroni 7:33).

Since there
is opposition in
all things, even as
there is faith, so must there
be its worldly counterpart. In
our day, the grip of fear paralyzes
many of God's children. Today, more
than ever, we need a hope in Christ. We
need the assurance of peace, that our
lives are moving in the direction
of our dreams, and that the
Atonement can help us
reach for the stars.

Faith is a
powerful financial
device that provides
over-draft protection as
we invest in the theater of
life. It stands as a guardian,
as a personal asset manager, to
make sure that we are not writing
checks along the way that cannot
later be cashed by a creditor who
goes by the name of Justice,
when our debts become
due and payable.

If we
wish to have
the faith to build
our own temples of
God, we must keep our
eyes fixed on the prize, as
we reach out beyond our
comfort zones, in order
to grasp the golden
ring on life's
carousel.

We are
lucky to have
been blessed with
the faith to be perfect
in Christ, and to become
witnesses of His power. We
are sanctified in Him by the
grace of God, and through
the shedding of His blood,
which is in the covenant
of the Father unto the
remission of our sins.
We are consecrated
to become holy
and without
spot.

We have
faith that
there is enough
room and enough
time in the eternities
for each of us develop
the capacity to see beyond
the limited horizon of our
vision all the way to the
Atonement that reaches
out to the best of us,
the worst of us, and
to everyone in
between.

In every age,
the tender shoots of
young testimony spring up
and are carefully nurtured in
accordance with Alma's inspired
formula, without the ecclesiastical
embroidery that too often needlessly
complicates the simple sewing, and
sowing, of Gospel messages.

As if they
were spiritual
swaddling clothes,
the fabric of faith that
has been integrated into
our coats of many colors
will resonate with intrinsic
light that betrays the fact
that its vibrancy can be
traced to more than
just pigment and
dye.

Belief is the mental assent to the truth of a precept, principle, or doctrine, without the moral element of responsibility that we call faith. Of those to whom much is given, however, much is expected. The gift of faith demands action. Therefore, when we exercise free will, even if we perform good works, without faith, it falls short. It "is dead, being alone." (James 2:17).

The Savior is our Advocate with the Father and is the Bread of Life, the foundation of faith beneath our existence, and the cornerstone of our belief. He is the Deliverer of the Everlasting Covenant and the Creator of worlds without number.

Faith
can vitalize
the moral fiber
that we need
to face our
demons.

If we want
to develop the
faith to choose the
harder right, instead
of the easier wrong, we
must begin by taking a
few confident steps into
the darkness. Only then
will its spiritual strong
searchlight illuminate
the way before us.

In matters of
faith, attitude is
all about altitude. We
must raise our sights, so
that we will always be
looking upward, in
the direction of
our dreams.

Faith
exposes us
to a constant
stream of insight,
intuition, inspiration
and revelation that flows
from above in a cascade of
creativity. A divine direction
dictates that we walk along
illuminated pathways as we
exercise our faculties of
mind and spirit.

Those
who are
firm in their
faith will find
that heaven will
come knocking
at their door.

Our attempts
to comprehend the
universe may help us
to understand ourselves.
If we ask, what is its origin,
or what is its ultimate destiny,
we are really asking where did we
come from, and where are we going.
When we discover the answers to these
questions, we will understand why we
are here, and we will be prepared to
embark upon the errand of the
Lord, which is the ultimate
incredible journey of
faith into the
future.

The
account of
the Creation that
was written by Moses
provided only the details
that relate to the Fall of Adam
and Eve, and to the Atonement of
Christ, which is the doctrine that we
must understand in order to have
the faith to live abundantly and
become heirs of salvation.

Pennies from heaven are as a dowry from Deity that is designed to foster our faith in the financial stability of His treasury and facilitate unwavering fidelity to the Savior of the world.

While they drew,
a kindergarten teacher
walked up and down the rows
in her classroom, observing her pupils'
work. She stopped at the desk of one little
girl and asked what her drawing was. She replied:
"I'm drawing a picture of God." The teacher paused,
and then tentatively said: "But no one knows what
God looks like." Without missing a beat or even
looking up from her paper, the girl said: "They
will in a minute." Though she was tender in
years, this child had faith.

Faith
asks a
lot. However,
it emboldens
us with hope, and
it blesses us with the
fortitude to be able to
endure. It motivates us to
seek after everything that is
lovely, or of good report,
or praiseworthy.

An unprincipled and faithless society deals with its spiritual myopia with a knee-jerk reaction that simply ratchets down its expectations. In the end, a society that lacks the fire of faith will ask very little of its members, and will receive in kind.

When we
look around
and realize that
we no longer believe,
the compromise of our
conversion can be attributed
to a lack of faithful focus that
initiated the flat spin from which we
could not recover. The blame for the
demolition of our discipleship, and
the chain-reaction of unfortunate
and inevitable consequences
that follows, is often laid
at the doorstep of
others.

Faith compels us
to trust God's divine
design rather than devilish
doctrines. It invites us to believe
that our lives are wonderful "fairy
tales waiting to be written by the
omnipotent hand of God."
(Hans Christian
Anderson).

When we maintain
the focus of our faith,
we don't get in the thick
of thin things. We cultivate
an equilibrium that is centered
far from the madding crowd, at a
safe distance from the ego-filled
minds of mediocre men. We are
insulated from the tumult, the
confusion, and the cares of
the world, and enjoy a
firmness that is
unshakable.

While they drew,
a kindergarten teacher
walked up and down the rows
in her classroom, observing her pupils'
work. She stopped at the desk of a little
girl and asked what her drawing was. She
replied: "I'm drawing a picture of God." Her
teacher tentatively said: "But no one knows
what God looks like." Without looking up
from her paper, the child said: "They will
in a minute." Though tender in years,
she had what we call "faith."

Those without
faith lack spiritual
horsepower. Their dearth
of traction is obvious, their
inability to generate spontaneity
is palpable, and their lack of energy
to engage enthusiasm is noticeable.
Their incapacity to spark vitality
is evident, and their failure to
candidly acknowledge the
powerful relationship that
can exist between God
and ourselves is
undisputed.

How we
develop the
faith to believe
will either deify us,
or it will destroy us, for
our response to the Savior
will delineate our dreams,
and define our destiny. It
will ultimately determine
how, where, and with
whom we will spend
all of eternity.

Faith
envelops us
in an intuitive
comprehension of
where we came from,
the tangible element of
why we are here, and the
revelatory reassurance we
need, to be at peace with
where we are going.

It is our faith that
teaches us to face the sun,
that we may feel the warmth
of its rays upon our cheeks, listen
with greater sensitivity, hear the word
of the Lord without ambiguity, and see
with a lucidity that encourages us to be
benevolently blind when we witness the
shortcomings of others who are at
different mile-posts on their
journey thru life.

Those of us
who have the faith to
become the beneficiaries
of God's divine intervention,
have been touched by angels,
are moved to compassion, or
have otherwise been blessed
to walk in the light
of the Lord.

When we think
of the multitude
of those angels who
are thinly disguised as
our families, friends, and
peers, who have helped us to
nurture our faith, we remember
the words of Sir Isaac Newton, who,
when pressed to reveal the secret
behind his accomplishments,
simply replied: "I stood
on the shoulders of
giants."

When
we enjoy
an unrestrained
rapport with God,
our faith to act will
generate the power to
"get things done" in an
expansive and interactive
way, in all holiness. We will
recognize His voice as Spirit,
and His Spirit as truth, which
"abideth and hath no end.
And if it be in (us) it
shall abound."
(D&C 88:66).

Our faith
puts the day to
day elements of The
Plan in perspective, that
we might more clearly be
able to distinguish the grey
-toned obstacles that lie in
our path. These barriers to our
progression will then stand out
in sharp contrast against the
polychromatic backdrop of
the design that God has
created for each
of us.

Knowledge
that has been
acquired through
the exercise of faith
is the mortar that binds
together the building
blocks of testimony
and conversion, as
as well as of hope
and charity.

Those who
have forsaken
the world and have
faithfully embraced the
lifestyle of Saints experience
nothing short of a spiritual heart
transplant. Therefore, anti-rejection
protocols must be followed after
we have spiritually been given
our new hearts and have
been born again.

The
second mile
of faith asks us to
shun telestial temptations
that are so cunningly peddled
by the snake oil salesmen who have
set up shop in the great and spacious
buildings that dot the landscapes
of our lives, and that pop up
in the most unexpected
places.

Paul painted a portrait of our second mile commitment of faith when he wrote: "Ye are manifestly declared to be the epistle of Christ ministered by us, written not with ink, but with the Spirit of the living God; (and not just) in tables of stone, but (also) in fleshy tables of the heart." (2 Corinthians 3:3).

As
we begin to
grasp the nature
of God, we learn more
about how we fit in to His
divine design. We learn how
faith can drive the law into
our inward parts. When it
does so, the articles of
our faith become the
particles of our
faith.

Those who have
partaken of the sweet,
sustaining influence of faith
have experienced a power that
stems from love, in contrast to
the Machiavellian influences
of lust and the unrighteous
desire for dominion.

Faith
blesses us
with a spiritual
"sixth sense" that
allows us to create
order amid chaos
and make sense
of creation.

Through the
workings of the
Spirit and by the power
of our faith, we see all the
way to heaven, with the capacity
to be carried beyond the perceptible
and palpable confines of this world
to a place where boundaries are
blurred, and the barricade of
borders evaporates in a
flood of light.

Faith guides us
with a star map that
has been created by the
hand of God to illuminate
the pathway to the promised
land. It is an endowment
of radiant light and
unearthly power.

Those who evince the nobility of faith may have been the first to comprehend the power behind the phrase: "Father knows best!"

Those with the nobility of faith fear no man, for they are as Bagheera, the powerfully built black panther in "The Jungle Book," who confided to Mowgli the man-cub: "I had never seen the jungle. They fed me behind bars from an iron pan till one night I felt that I was Bagheera the Panther, and no man's plaything, and I broke the lock with one blow of my paw and came away." (Rudyard Kipling).

The effects of sin are inevitable and inescapable, but for the intercession of faith in the Atonement. The Maker and Fashioner of the universe must intervene by engaging laws that restore equilibrium, or all is lost. In the heavens, there is a "better and an enduring substance." (Hebrews 10:34).

The
tendency
toward turmoil
lies in wait to disrupt
the poise of those who are
pressing forward toward
the divine center
of faith.

There is no
variability in
the divine center
of faith. We simply
trust the Savior, when
He reassures us: "I am
the way, the truth, and
the life. No man cometh
unto the Father, but by
me." (John 14:6).

Ever since the Fall, Satan has enjoyed a free pass to mingle among the children of men. This flushes him with excitement, because he knows how difficult it is for us to resist a natural tendency toward volatility. Those who love Satan more than they love God unavoidably exhibit the behavioral manifestations of that misplaced adoration.

Those of little faith characteristically throw up defensive dross that is designed to deflect, disrespect, disregard, discourage, or disparage the uncomfortably penetrating question: "What think ye of Christ?"

There will come
for each of us a great
and dreadful day when we
will be asked to stand and give
our sworn deposition before God,
angels, and witnesses. On the issue
of faith, depending upon our answer,
we will be counted among the sheep
or the goats, and find ourselves
on His right hand or on His
left hand.

Faith
blesses us
to become fluent
in a heavenly language
that is rhythmical, melodious,
soothing to our ears, and calming
to our souls. When we hear the Spirit
quietly whisper: "You're a stranger here,"
we are comforted with the realization
that we have "wandered from a
more exalted sphere."
(Eliza R. Snow).

Without knowledge, there can be no faith; without faith, there can be no light, and without light there can be no recognition of religious truth; and without spiritual enlightenment, if just one of the three elements of faith, light, and truth is lost, then all must be forsaken. Our fortunes rest on the basis of how completely we have embraced the knowledge of faith.

We
who have
the faith to
be born again
are set free by the
perfect Law of Liberty
to reach our potential.
We are as the acorns of
mighty oaks, vitalized by
faith and basking in the
nurturing influence of
God to grow to the
full stature of
our spirits.

Joseph Smith understood the energy of faith when he prayed: "Help us by the power of thy Spirit, that we may mingle our voices with those bright, shining seraphs around thy throne, with acclimations of praise, singing Hosanna to God and the Lamb!" (D&C 109:79).

Without faith and knowledge, the children of men find that they are caught up in a flat spin from which there is no recovery.

Sooner or later,
every member of the
Church will encounter
a line drawn in the sand.
Those who have the faith to
"endure unto the end, the
same shall be saved."
(Matthew 24:13).

Our faith
pushes us toward
perfection, which often
means that we persevere to
the point that we feel that we
have no more to give. It is at the
point of utter exhaustion that we
must turn to powers that are
greater than ourselves, if
we hope to survive
the ordeal.

Our faith
is a tool that
allows us to see
beyond the limited
horizon of our sight,
to be touched by a vision
of the virtue of the word of
God. Our faith enables us to
savor revealed truth with a
discriminating taste that
discerns the distinctive
flavor of eternal
worlds.

We live in the
midst of Spiritual
Babylon, and recoil as
we encounter a sprawling
wasteland of worldliness that
reeks of the rotting stench of sin.
But we must not allow our faith
to be contaminated by the raw
sewage that is unleashed by
Satan's servants, who are
often thinly disguised
as sanitation
workers.

Those who
were denied the
chance in this life to
embrace the Gospel will be
judged according to their more
limited understanding of the doctrines
and principles of God's Plan. Therefore,
when they approach the Bar of Justice, they
will necessarily vary in their accountability
to law. Therein lies the hidden power of the
Gospel to ultimately bless our lives, without
regard to our individual circumstances.
We play the hand we have been
dealt, as best we can.

As we gain spiritual maturity by doing our duty, our faith increases until it becomes perfect knowledge.

As imperfect mortals who are struggling to believe what we do not see, the reward of our maturing faith is to see what we believe. Some things just have to be believed to be seen, until our faith in Jesus Christ has been perfected.

At times
of weakness, it
may seem to us that the
easier way out is to adopt
the ways of the world, and that
it is harder to acknowledge that
there is an autobiographical thread
within each of us that leads all the
way back to heaven. Sometimes,
we cannot see the forest for
the trees, and we forget
that the universe is a
machine for the
making of
gods.

If we
allow ourselves
to succumb to fear,
and permit faithlessness
to handcuff the expression
of our choices, often all that is
left in the end is a monochromatic
and one-dimensional compromise
that leaves us with a hollow core
of emptiness in the pit of our
stomachs and terror in our
hearts. Faith, after all, is
fear that has said
its prayers.

Faith commits
us to the arduous
process of spiritual
rebirth that accompanies
choosing the harder right,
rather than capitulating to
the character-crippling
miscarriage of the
easier wrong.

Our faith
charges the air
in the theater of life
as fire in the sky, with an
electricity that represents the
inevitable merger of the universal
encouragement of the Light of
Christ with the pointed and
providential guidance of
the Holy Ghost.

The cohesive influence of the mighty foundation of faith creates an effectual bridge of understanding that spans the gap between heaven and earth.

It seems
clear that our faith
should remain fixed upon
the revelations the Lord has
given us that relate to our world,
and not on mysteries that have not
been revealed to us, may never be
revealed, or that just may not
be pertinent to our current
circumstances.

When we
have stockpiled
ample reserves in
our spiritual savings
accounts, when they are
nearing depletion, or even
if our accounts are overdrawn,
in every case we still receive
pennies from heaven, or
the currency of faith
in its myriad
forms.

Our faith
blesses us with a
pure form of focus,
transforming our five
natural senses into something
wonderful by a heaven-sent sixth
sense that defies description. Physical
and spiritual resources work in tandem
to compound each other, and to condition
us through the patience of faith, the miracle
of repentance, the diligence of baptism,
the sweet spirit of the Holy Ghost, and
an exhilarating renewal in the
Sacrament.

We don't
intend to lose our
faith. It is only that our
conviction just fades away
like a slow leak in an
automobile tire, rather
than as a sudden
blowout.

The activities
in which the unfaithful
are engaged do not require
commitment to a belief, but only
minimal effort, little responsibility, and
virtually no accountability. Someone once
said that the Lord gave us two ends: one to
think with and the other to sit on. Which
one we use will determine how well
we do in life. In other words:
Heads we win, and tails
we lose.

Focused faith
"generates power, for
a mind once stretched by
a new idea can never return
to its original dimension."
(Oliver Wendell Holmes).

Faith steps up and helps us, as we catalyze our feeling, capture our emotion, contour our attitude, crystallize thought, congeal passion, compartmentalize action and convey sentiment, that lead to spiritual revitalization.

Faith prompts
us to examine what
it means to be anxiously
engaged, inspires us to plumb
the depths of our commitment to
the Savior, sensitizes us to the nobility
of His work, expands upon His visions of
immortality, personalizes the Atonement,
and helps us to remain consciously
aware of our close proximity
to heaven.

The courage
of faith can be
the catalyst that
transforms timidity
into powerful presence
of mind. Thereby, is
created a platform
for assertive
action.

When
we express
ourselves through
positive and independent
action, the courage of faith
introduces us to the exhilarating
emotion and feeling of freedom
from incarceration to sin that we
can only experience when we
have been obedient to a
Higher Power.

Our faith points us to doctrine, so that when we encounter the principles of The Plan, we will respond to the truth with actions that have both the form and the substance of a godly walk, and that boldly testify of His power to save.

Unpretentious
professors of faith
are not easily swayed
by conventional wisdom
or by politically expedient
ideology, and they remain
uninfluenced by shifting
sands of secularism or
by situational ethics.

It is heartbreaking when
those who have matriculated
in the curriculum of the Gospel,
but cannot sustain saving faith, set
their sights too low, too easily reaching
watered-down objectives. They no longer
stretch themselves, and rarely venture out
of the comfort zones to which they have
retreated. They have little to show for
the consistently timid efforts that
deny the faith but have become
habitual in their expression.

Modern scribes and Pharisees who have little or no faith omit the weightier matters of the law. They strain at a gnat, and swallow a camel. They appear to be righteous, but inside are "full of extortion and excess." (Matthew 23:25). Our righteous desire to choose with the wisdom of faith brings us closer to the Lord Jesus Christ, leaving no room for hypocrisy to creep into our lives.

The second mile
of faith asks us to
forge a spiritual bond
with our fellow travelers
by obedience that is more
expansive than a law of
carnal commandments.
It requires the inter-
dependency of
the greater
law.

Those
who live by faith
embrace the Gospel
because its teachings
express a crystal clear
perspective as a pattern
of heaven is traced out
by the finger of God,
using the fabric of a
telestial tapestry.

Faith
caresses
our spirits with
inexplicable images
of religious recognition
that remind us of our
noble birthright.

Faith
establishes
the boundaries
of heaven, and puts
them beyond the reach
of detection by even the
most sophisticated and
accurately calibrated
instruments utilized
by our terrestrial
scientists.

There will
come a day
for the faithful
when the sun shall
not go down, "neither
shall the moon withdraw
itself. For the Lord shall be
their everlasting light."
(Isaiah 60:20).

If we do not
acknowledge the
stability of the divine
center of faith, and expend
energy to cultivate its sense of
permanency, everything tends
to collapse into disarray.

The Law
of Eternal
Progression
rules supreme,
but it is defined
by its opposites in
the physical universe
just as it is by the forces
of opposition in the eternal
world. Satan's presence in
the Garden of Eden
attests to that
fact.

While faith nurtures the
development of personality
traits that are in concordance
with the symmetry of heaven, sin
is harmful because it destroys our
ability to nurture the equilibrium
that is a defining characteristic
of those who inherit eternal
life. In God's nature, there
is neither variableness,
nor shadow of
turning.

We trust
our divine
center and we
understand how
our disposition to
draw upon our faith
can be stimulating and
even enlightening.

Adam and Eve
fell that they and
their posterity might
know true happiness, and
nurture the moral fiber that
we recognize today as saving
faith. They were given the tools
they would need to consistently
choose the harder right, instead
of the easier wrong, that they
might find that happiness
that has been prepared
for the Saints of
God.

The Plan
was carefully
crafted to create
the conditions wherein
we might be prompted and
strengthened by the Light of
Christ, that we might choose the
harder right; that, in faith, we
might make the most of the
cradle and crucible of
our experience.

If we want
to develop the
faith to choose the
harder right, instead
of the easier wrong, we
must expend soul-sweat. As
Robert Frost wrote: "I shall be
telling this with a sigh somewhere
ages and ages hence: Two roads
diverged in a wood, and I took
the one less traveled by, and
that has made all the
difference."

Faith provides us with a
regularly recurring reassurance
of a religious recalibration that auto
corrects with a celestial precision. Faith
envelops us in an intuitive appreciation of
where we came from, why we are here, and
where we are going. It gives us the courage
to face the future with confidence and
to maintain our forward momentum
during the journey so we won't
lose our balance, fall down,
and possibly injure our
divine nature.

As
our circle
of knowledge
expands, so will the
borders separating the
kernels of wisdom that we
have grasped, from a yet
undiscovered country.
It seems that the
more we know,
the more we
need to
learn.

The Lord
created the earth
as a testing center, a
learning laboratory, a
citadel of higher education,
a place where we would be given
all the tools that could conceivably
be necessary to validate God's faith
in us, and to see if we might muster
an equivalent faith, to be proven
to be worthy of His trust.

Wo unto those
who only casually
receive the illumination
of faith in God that has been
so freely given. Because of their
misguided obsession with temporal
trivia, they carelessly fritter away
their faith, and waste the days of
their probation rooting through
telestial trash in a fruitless
effort to find meaning
in their empty lives.

In a
vain attempt
to avoid societal
implosion, and for
the sake of cultural
expediency, the target has
been moved so many times
to score repetitive bulls-eyes,
that no-one will concede that
it is the arrow of faith that
has strayed far from
the mark.

Our best intentions may be noble, but vision without work is dreamery, and even if we work hard, without vision, it is drudgery. If we focus our faith and work with vision, however, it will be our destiny to soar with eagles, rather than walk with turkeys.

During our
journey of faith,
we use the talents we
have been given, knowing
that the woods would be very
quiet if no birds sang except
those that sang best.

When the Pharisees gathered together, Jesus asked them if they would put their money where their faith was. He asked them, "What think ye of Christ?" and "Whose son is he?" (Matthew 22:41).

Our faith
provides a shield
of protection against
the corrosive spatter of
perspiration cast off by the
destroyer, who pervasively and
persistently is working overtime to
damage our doctrinal defenses, dull
our spiritual sensitivities, diminish
our charitable capacity, deplete
our bountiful reservoirs of
sympathy, and destroy
our devotions.

When we feel
the urge to push
the Lord's agenda,
faith can be our labor
coach, providing us with
just the right amount of
encouragement we need
to successfully deliver
our witness without
being overbearing.

Guidance from above that
comes to us in the form of spiritual
promptings and subtle impressions are more
common that many would suspect. There are
powerful intuitive communicators that strongly
influence nearly all of us to push forward in
the direction of our dreams, toward a faith
to believe that blesses us with a greater
appreciation of the concern of
our Creator for each of us.

As we nurture
our faith, we realize how
heavily we have borrowed from
the towering examples of those who,
over the years, have been our mystical
mentors, our sensible chaperones, our
compassionate critics, our spiritual
guides, our surrogate saviors,
and our divine teachers
incarnate.

As
we consider
the performance
potential of faith,
we remember that it
is not our purpose to
be stars of the show. A
pathway of progress may
lead us in the direction
of perfection, but it is a
process, rather than a
point. We will not be
given, nor will we
need, top billing
to realize our
dreams.

No wonder that it is the priest's duty to preach, teach, expound, exhort, and to baptize, as well as to administer the sacrament. (See D&C 20:46). Their awesome responsibility is to speak with faith by the power of the Holy Ghost as if their voices were the Lord's own voice, and then to follow up their words with actions.

In a perfect
storm of knowledge,
belief, and faith, it is the
light of faith that switches on
as a bright star in the heavens
whose hydrogen fuel powers
the chain reaction of its
nuclear furnace.

Exalting faith
has the capacity to
become the fundamental
element of a tapestry whose
intricate design will reveal itself,
in all its glory, as an expression of
our being. When we attain the full
stature of our spirits because our
nature has finally conformed to
the harmony of heaven, our
perfect frames will burst
free of the shackles of
our mortal clay, as
vibrant coats of
many colors.

Similar to a
dialysis machine, the
ordinance of the Sacrament
is a mechanism that removes
impurities from our hearts, so
that we might have the faith
necessary to build the holy
accommodations that are
worthy of the habitation
of our spirits.

While
the desire to
obtain gold can
certainly corrupt us,
the bright, shiny metal
that cannot be corroded
symbolizes the purity that
turns our thoughts to, and
concentrates our faith on,
the inestimable worth of
the Celestial Kingdom
whose gilded streets
must be dazzling
to the eye.

The
legal
tender of
believing faith
is the currency we
all need, to purchase
the Golden Tickets
for our passage
Home.

As
long as we
remain in a state
of rebellion against the
Spirit, the fruit of the tree
of life will remain just beyond
our reach, even if out of curiosity,
we now and then attempt to take a
bite. If we never raise our eyes to
search eternal horizons, the world
before us will appear as nothing
more than a barren desert that
is devoid of refreshing oases,
the welcome shade of trees,
and an abundance of well
watered gardens. If we
lack enough faith to
nourish the word,
its living water
cannot sustain
us.

"We, having the same spirit of faith, according as it is written, I believed, and therefore, have I spoken; we also believe, and therefore, speak." (2 Corinthians 4:13).

Those
with faith to
choose the harder
right, instead of the
easier wrong, will distain
Babylons' amusement parks,
while gratefully utilizing the
aid stations that have been
providentially positioned
all over Zion, and in
particular, at the
Sacrament
table.

When the
Light of Christ
and the Holy Ghost
streak in tandem across
the heavens, it is easy for us
to follow in faith its flaming
trajectory. It traces its way
across a cosmic ocean
that radiates with
luminosity.

It may be
our faith that
causes our blood to
run hot, reminiscent of
the microwave background
radiation from the creation
of our universe that occurred
billions of years ago, and of
the creation of the Garden
of Eden, that was not so
very long ago.

By allowing
ourselves to be
habitually distracted
by trifling concerns until
they become the center of our
attention and even our obsession,
we ignore our innate yearning to
exercise faith in God, and we
thereby commit a grievous
sin of omission.

With faith, we focus on what we want to happen, instead of allowing ourselves to be distracted by what we don't want to happen. We have envisioned success so many times, that the conclusion is foregone. We must succeed and it is inevitable that we will prevail. It is our destiny to dance with the stars.

Paul exhorted the Philippian Saints to work out their salvation with fear and trembling. He knew that if they put their hearts and their souls into the effort, it would leave them physically and spiritually exhausted. Still, he invited them to join him as he pressed "toward the mark, for the prize of the high calling of God in Christ Jesus." (Philippians 3:14).

When we have
been reintroduced
to the noble principles
that guided us through our
spiritual kindergarten years in
the pre-earth existence, we are
blessed with the focus of faith
to accompany us during the
return to our more natural
state of harmony with
the heavens.

Paul observed of the Athenians, who were similar in many ways to us, that they were inclined to bow down before the unknown gods whom they worshipped in ignorance.

To
avoid the
fate of those who
greet the Gospel with
skepticism, and to insure
that our faith is animated
with energy, and so that we
will have no regrets, we have
been given, not only the Light
of Christ, but also the gift
of the Holy Ghost.

Faith makes
it easier to have
bowels that have been
moved to compassion for
those who are struggling
with misfortune or the
heavy weight of
unresolved
sin.

The more we
think about Christ,
the easier it is to craft
with words the sensations
that naturally flow to each
of us as a result of the stirrings
of the Spirit. It becomes that much
easier to generate, and sustain,
the faith to believe in the
Father, the Son, and
the Holy Ghost.

We dream that we might feel the gentle caress of the Master's hand, as our spiritual muscles are massaged by faith. We want Him to mold us and shape us as the Artisan of our destiny.

Our faith
elicits displays
of celestial energy
worthy of notice from
above. As fire in the sky,
the air in the theater of life
is charged with an electricity
that is the sum of the merger of
the universal encouragement of
the Light of Christ, together with
the pointed and providential
guidance provided by
the Holy Ghost.

Armed with faith,
our innermost longings
to apprehend visions of the
eternal world are epitomized
by our triumphant realization of
dreams fulfilled. In the expression
of our testimonies, our emotions are
painted by words that depict our
progression toward the distant
mileposts that mark the way
we must all follow as we
journey to heaven.

When we find ourselves hesitantly inching our way thru life, faith invigorates us with renewed energy, and instills within us the desire to redouble our efforts to maintain the integrity of our testimonies.

Who would
consciously choose to
lead a marginalized life, or
to become spiritually depleted
on a personal or an institutional
level? We perish because our faith has
failed us. But how many of us have the
courage to realize that it is the other
way around; that it is we who have
failed our faith? Fortunately, if
we are blessed with the gift
of time, we can change
all that, beginning
right now.

There is a pulsing arpeggio entitled "Faith to Believe" that ignites our souls with passion. It is this catalyzing influence that was conspicuously missing from the pedantic charade of righteous behavior that was embraced by the Pharisees of old, and that is absent in so many circles even today.

Our
faith helps to
reacquaint us with
a divine design as we
put the finishing touches on
our dissertation on life. As we
are perfected, our composition
will be recognized for what it
has become: a true magnum
opus, even God's work
and glory.

Is it easier to go with the flow, and harder to swim against the current, or easier to walk with turkeys, and harder to soar with eagles?

When we
think as adults, and
put away childish things, we
sacrifice to a degree our ability
to express ourselves naturally,
with unrestrained spontaneity.
Similarly, if we stop seeing
the world through the eye
of faith, we can lose
our joie de
vivre.

Without faith, we
strangle ourselves with
material things whose opacity
obstructs our ability to see how
God has so thoughtfully laid out
before us the smorgasbord of
life, and has invited us to
freely partake of
its delights.

John F. Kennedy famously declared: "We choose to do things, not because they are easy, but because they are hard. Our goals will serve to organize and measure the best of our energies and skills. Our challenges are those that we are willing to accept, and that we are unwilling to postpone, but that we intend to win." That is well put, but we must never forget that one plus God equals a majority. We need to keep the faith!

Hidden within
the fabric of The Plan
of Salvation is a Golden
Ticket that bestows upon each
of us the means to claim the
blessings of heaven if we but
endure to the end in faith,
while we yet dwell on
the earth.

Faith to go the
second mile focuses
our discipleship on the
commandment to be willing
to mourn with those who mourn,
and to comfort those that stand
in need, and to be witnesses of
God, wherever we may be,
for as long as we
shall live.

Sometimes, those who surrender their dreams and their faith sell their birthright to the lowest bidder for a mess of pottage. Once they have made the exchange, they may far too easily be dragged down to a hell on earth where they realize that the prison into which they have been cast was of their own construction.

Even with the aid of
the world's most powerful
telescopes, and notwithstanding
the Light of Christ, we have been
privileged only to take a peek
at the creations Moses beheld
through the mighty power of
faith, and while under
the influence of the
Holy Ghost.

When we
encounter truth,
our sinews will resonate
with recognition. Ultimately,
every one who hearkens to
the voice of the Spirit will
eventually come unto
God, even our
Father.

Society pays
a heavy price when it
lacks a faithful focus on
the solemnities of eternity.
For example, when its spiritual
equilibrium has become disoriented
and its moral compass is spinning out
of control, its values are quickly adjusted
in a misguided, vain, and even unconscious
attempt to regain a state of balance
with the order of heaven.

The faithful find mentors whom they can emulate, instead of scapegoats that are easy to blame. Instead of looking for easier answers, they dig deeply to uncover healthier solutions to the problems they face.

By using specifically authorized and sanctioned words, we exercise the faith to perform ordinances ranging from baptisms to the sealing ordinances of the temple.

It is
interesting to
think of Joseph's
coat of many colors
as a metaphor for the
fabric of our faith, sewn
by our Heavenly Father. We
can visualize how each thread
has been individually tailored to
suit our circumstances; to represent,
not the drab monotone of the world,
but a true Technicolor DreamCoat
signifying the glories and riches
of dazzling eternal worlds.

When we
walk in the
light of life and
go out of our way to
grasp the principles of truth,
we brim over with gratitude as
we discover how our Redeemer has
provided luxurious accommodations
for us in the household of faith.

Our faith
allow us to
free ourselves
from the mire of
sin, and to cleanse
ourselves in the blood
of Jesus Christ; to stand
steadily upon Gospel sod.
Our faith separates us from
those who precariously hop
about on the flotsam and
the jetsam that bobs up
and down and tosses
to and fro, on the
unpredictable sea
of life.

With
simple faith,
we press on in
the Light of Christ,
and are rewarded with
an illumination of Gospel
principles that bathes our
minds in a cascade of
inspiration and
revelation.

Faith is impotent when it does not lead to purposeful performance. It is the sizzle without the steak. Real faith involves a vital, personal self-commitment to a practical belief. But at the end of the day, our good works lack the efficacy for salvation. What makes us good is faith in Christ, and faith in Christ activates God's grace in our behalf.

We prepare
to embrace our
faith by practicing
fast-scale runs through
more than half a dozen
octaves on all 88 of the
glistening black and
white ivory keys
of experience.

Faith
nudges us off
our complacency
plateaus, as we steer
away from the trendy
cafés situated along the
broad avenues of Idumea.
We are transported as on the
wings of eagles beyond the
boundaries of our self-
imposed limitations
along a highway
that leads to
heaven.

It is our faith that our children are the living messages we send to a time we will not see.

Adults who have
learned to swim with
sharks are characterized
as "seasoned veterans" and
yet the process fails to tenderize
them. Instead, it curses them with a
thick skin containing precious few
sensory nerve endings to leave
room for the nurturing
of their faith.

Faith extends to us the promise of a wonderful opportunity to enjoy the bliss of our heavenly home. It is there, that we will enjoy the warm embrace of our Father, His Son, Jesus Christ, and the Holy Ghost.

If
we try
to shirk the
demands of faith,
we will be swallowed
up by a leviathan no less
real than that of Jonah, and
we will eventually be spit out
upon the rocky shoreline of
our obligations.

Blessed are they who, when they face temptation, have the faith to turn to the right. They shall avoid telestial traffic jams and doctrinal detours.

Faith, light, and truth may be recognized as irreducible common denominators. They are the essential elements of an equation that describes the foundation upon which knowledge is received. "One for all and all for one!" was the motto of the Three Musketeers. Without faith, light, and truth, said Joseph Smith, we would "degenerate from God, descend to the devil, and lose knowledge."

If the octane rating of the fuel that fires our faith to build our temples of God is too low, we may be able to just barely get by, but only for a time. As we limp along with our engines misfiring badly, our fear will ultimately overpower our faith.

Jesus
utilized
the tools
that nurture
the dependent
inter-relationship
between our physical
and spiritual well-being
and obedience, as we all
must do if we wish to enjoy
the faith to follow His divine
design during the construction
of our mortal tabernacles that
were envisioned by God to
become the holy temples
of our spirits.

Faith is more than our intellectual assent. Its influence extends as far as our deeds. Therefore, works become an important companion to vital, active faith.

During the
genesis of our faith, it
is necessary for us to take
a few steps into the darkness,
in order to let the spiritual strong
searchlight of truth illuminate the
way. Only after the trial of our
faith, will it be confirmed by
the Spirit that God is both
its Author and Finisher.
He has us covered
coming and
going.

If we want
to develop the
faith to choose the
harder right, instead
of the easier wrong, we
will maintain unbridled
optimism, and we will be
consumed, as it were, by
a divine fire. We will
be faithful, or full
of faith.

As in a heavenly language
that is rhythmical, melodious,
soothing to our ears, and calming
to our souls, we hear the Spirit quietly
whisper: "You're a stranger here." We are
immediately comforted by the realization
that we have "wandered from a more
exalted sphere." (Eliza R. Snow).

"Happiness is the object and design of our existence. It will be the end thereof, if we follow the path that leads to it; and that path is virtue, uprightness, faithfulness, holiness, and keeping all the commandments of God." (Joseph Smith).

Faith carries
us in positive and
meaningful ways to
green pastures where we
enjoy the warm embrace of
the Good Shepherd, and where
we are permitted to experience
the intimacy of the touch of His
garment, even if we sometimes
feel that we have been lost
in the press of the crowd
within the sheepfold.

When we feel
the energy of faith
building within us, we
realize that it can lift us
to the zenith of experience,
until the lines distinguishing
mortality from eternity blur.
At that moment, when we find
ourselves in a condition that,
for the lack of better words,
can only be described as if
we were being born again,
we will be consumed in
a fire of everlasting
burnings.

The stern warning: "Wait until your father gets home!" applies equally to children and to adults. It makes us turn our thoughts to the reunion we will one day have with Deity, when we will be invited to explain our behavior before the Judgment Bar of Christ.

Our
faith reflects
enduring qualities
that are the embodiment
of our Parents' nurturing
influence. We see others as
neighbors and not strangers.
We are less judgmental and
are more accepting of our
differences. We are less
suspicious and are
friendlier.

No
matter
in what
direction
we face, we
will always feel
the presence of the
Lord, for He will be
before our faces,
forever and a
day.

We have
faith that Jesus
is the Father of our
spiritual regeneration,
and like the parent we all
aspire to be, He will be there
to bind our wounds and heal
our infirmities every time we
stumble and whenever we fall
because of the weight we have
been trying to carry all by
ourselves. Even though we
may forget all about the
Atonement, the Savior
will never forget
about us.

The
masses
settle for
mediocrity,
while once in
a while, one or
two faithful souls
forget themselves
into heaven.

Our society, which is arguably good, has failed miserably to instill faith in the rising generation. When a culture believes that truth is relative and that the merits of faith are arbitrarily determined, the stage is set for a temporal and spiritual disaster of biblical proportion.

The world seeks change by exerting external control, and fails miserably. The Savior seeks change by transforming the inner vessel, and succeeds brilliantly. He does this by calibrating our internal compass so that we remain oriented toward the discipline of faith.

In the Standard Works, we are urged 129 times to learn, 154 times to be perfect, and 306 times to be obedient, but 995 times to begin. Now is the time that we must begin to exercise saving faith in God.

We know that
God is sensitive
to our needs, because
He has taught us just how
powerful our effectual and
fervent prayers can be. When we
are in conformity to the laws of
heaven, we draw virtue from a
life force that is the Spirit of
God. We have figuratively
reached out and touched
the hem of the Savior's
garment, even if we
are in the press of
the crowd.

Faithful disciples of Christ are able to clearly identify the fingerprints of Satan, because they have been smeared all over a plethora of penurious programs, policies, politics, and parties that do little more than to promote personal and provincial proclamations relating to plans that are, at best, petty.

No matter how
wide the net is cast,
science cannot explain
the flickering shadows of
eternity that dance all around
us, as the familiar features of
mortality are illuminated for
all of the children of God
to see, by the brightly
burning light of
faith.

The Spirit confirms our faith to see all the way to heaven, and responds to our inquiry: "O God, where art thou, and where is the pavilion that covereth thy hiding place?" (D&C 121:1).

Our faith
introduces us
to a ladder that
has been set up on
the earth, the top of
which reaches all
the way to
heaven.

Faith is an engine that can only operate between the hot reservoir of the Son and the cold reaches of outer space.

To successfully
complete the curriculum
of the Gospel and graduate
with honors from the school of
hard knocks, we must first
have given our language
to the exhortation
of faith.

As we profess our faith, the Lord encourages us to move forward, but not in the press of a crowd that jostles for position in the three-ring circus of doctrinal dead ends, conceptual cul de sacs, and telestial trivialities.

Wo unto those
who groan under
darkness and under
the bondage of sin. They
squander precious resources
groping about in a frantic but
fruitless search for meaning in
their lives. In short, they fail to
appreciate the stabilizing power
that could have been theirs if
they had only focused on
the soothing influence
of faith.

Many of those who have lost their faith and have wandered into disbelief have done so because they have deferred or deterred their response to the question: "Whose son is this Jesus of Nazareth?"

When our faith
is focused, we know
how to worship and we
know what to worship, for
truth may be recognized by
its effects. We test the claims
of the Gospel by rendering
unswerving obedience to
its principles of
action.

Our focused faith protects
us from a false sense of carnal
security, as well as from indifferent
complacency. We view our weaknesses
in positively constructive ways, and are
grateful for our conscious awareness of
opportunities for personal improvement,
and for the tools that we have been
given to accomplish our mortal
mission assignments.

At the most basic level, idleness is the devil's workshop, and so our refusal to exercise our faith is sin. It is wasting our precious resources in fruitless pursuits, when we should have been engaged in other and better activities for which we have been blessed with God-given talents and capabilities.

Hope is the
inevitable result
of well-founded faith,
when we are meek and
lowly of heart, and are in
control of our desires and
emotions; when our appetites
and behavior lie within the
bounds established
by the Lord.

It is nothing
less than our faith
that binds together the
building blocks of eternal
principles. Without faith, the
fabric of our lives unravels in a
process leading to disintegration.
When the anchor of the knowledge
of faith is absent, our experiences
can be like a train wreck in slow
motion that is frustratingly
repeated over and over.

If we were
permitted to look
with the eye of faith
thru a spiritual prism,
we would be able to see
beyond the limited horizon
of our sight, all the way into
eternity. Through the power of
the Spirit, our eyes would be
opened to understand the
things of God.

One exciting element of well-founded faith is the stream of inspiration and revelation that cascades down from above. This insures that we walk along illuminated pathways leading to the only institution that may legitimately claim inspiration from divine guidance.

It is our faith that makes it easier to have hands that are accustomed to lifting those who need our support, and feet that are quick to carry us to those who have become imprisoned by poor choices or bad habits, or hobbled by ruinous circumstances.

When, in our
expressions of faith,
our passion clouds our
vision or overpowers our
zealous intentions, or if the
syntax of our speech seems too
bland or too spicy, if our feelings
are overstated, or if we are given over
to hyperbole, or even if we appear to drift
over the line separating true doctrine
from baseless speculation, we ask
the forgiving indulgence of
our Father in Heaven.

The cohesive
influence of the
mighty foundation
of faith creates bridges
of understanding between
the secular and the divine.
Life, with all its twists and
turns, and its permutations
and combinations, suddenly
makes more sense, as we
begin to understand
the mind and will
of God.

We
watch ourselves
judiciously, and are
the meticulous guardians
of our thoughts, the scrupulous
custodians of our words, and the
prudent caretakers of our actions.
We fastidiously observe the laws of
God, that we might benefit from the
stability of a pathway that basks in
the steady illumination that is
generously provided by the
discipline of faith.

As we endure
in faith, precious
emanations of familiar
and soothing oscillations
of energy that resonate from
within the limitless reserves of
the Spirit will be selflessly shared
by the Holy Ghost, Who will carry us
along on rolling waves of revelation
toward a shoreline of stability that
nurtures a sure and abiding
witness of the Savior's
divinity.

Faith carries us to the edge of eternity, to the very portals of heaven, where "forever" stands revealed in a mind bending panorama that lies before us.

God has creatively cultivated our capacity, through faith, to recapture the wide-eyed wonder and innocence of our youth.

The enlightening provisions of faith reintroduce us to our childhood, and give us a second chance to get it right.

It is
because
of our faith
that we can rely
upon the horns of
sanctuary, to grasp
them whenever our
yoke seems too
heavy for us
to bear
alone.

It makes no
difference if we
turn to the right or
to the left, because the
Savior is always there. When
we lift our eyes to the heavens,
He is watching us from above. No
matter that we bear the weight of
sin or sorrow with downcast eyes;
He is always beneath us, to lift
us up and carry our burdens.
Each time we knock, He
answers. Each time we
ask, we receive.

As Moroni taught: "Whoso believeth in Christ, doubting nothing, whatsoever he shall ask the Father in the name of Christ it shall be granted him; and this promise is unto all" who have the faith to properly prepare. (Mormon 9:21).

The Law
of the Lord
lies at the heart
of the foundation
principles that shape
our mortal mission,
guide its progress,
and guarantee
its success.

Is it
easier to yield
to temptation, and
harder to resist sin? Is
rebellion an easier option, and
obedience a more difficult choice?
Is it easier to live in a confusing fog
of conflicting values, and harder to
be guided, in faith, by tablets of
stone, and by what our Father
in Heaven has written with
His finger on the fleshy
tables of our
hearts?

The process
by which our faith
is strengthened is one
that tests the mettle of our
convictions. The Savior will not
cause us to misplace our trust, or our
confidence, in anything that cannot deliver
on its promises, but we have no proof until
we act on the basis of faith. Then comes
confirmation of the reality, as feelings
of self-assuredness grow and our
purposeful actions replace
tentative overtures.

Once
we have
received
the anointing
of faith, we will
not be able to rest
"until the last enemy
is conquered, death is
destroyed, and truth
reigns triumphant."
(Parley P. Pratt).

To each one
of us "there comes
in their lifetime that special
moment when they are figuratively
tapped on the shoulder and offered a
chance to do a very special thing, unique
to them and fitted to their talents. What a
tragedy if that moment finds them
unprepared or unqualified for
that which could have been
their finest hour."
(Churchill).

Faithful professors
exemplify themselves
as independent witnesses.
Memorable professors move
beyond good intentions that
are nothing but dreams, while
visionary professors back up
their words with deeds
that give life to
desire.

Humble
professors of
faith are guided
by the Spirit. Idealistic
professors are greater than
managers; they lead by example.
Purposeful professors help others
to clarify their own feelings.
Their guidance is founded
on principles, rather
than on values.

Firm professors refuse to accept mediocrity in their lives; instead they strive to align their behavior and their faith so that both are in harmony with the word of God, as well as with His nature.

Our capacity for decisive action has been designed so that it might increase over time as it is guided by the discipline of faith.

When
we are under
the influence of
the Spirit, we speak
of principles in such a
way that those of faltering
faith are encouraged to take
their first tentative steps toward
commitment, while, simultaneously,
more spiritually mature disciples, as
they realize that present levels of
performance are not acceptable,
are inspired to lengthen their
stride as they walk the
second mile.

Is it easier to throw in the towel and give up, and harder to push on, and continue the good fight? Is it easy to settle for average, and difficult to become exceptional? Those of faith willingly accept these challenges, not because they are easy, but precisely and pointedly because they are hard.

In harmony
with the principle
of opposition in all
things, an impenetrable
veil has been drawn across
our minds. But we have the Light
of Christ, and even the witness of the
Holy Ghost, to help us to penetrate that
curtain. Nevertheless, many of us are still
swayed by the siren song of Satan, drawn
to his duplicitous shoals of spiritual
instability, thereon to founder, and
to be pulled under by the riptides
of religious relativism and the
undertow of agnosticism, or
faithless skepticism.

We rely upon the strength of our faith, when we wonder, as did Paul: "O the depth of the riches both of the wisdom and the knowledge of God! How unsearchable are his judgments, and his ways past finding out! For who hath known the mind of the Lord? Or who hath been his counsellor?" (Romans 11:33-34).

When the Spirit nurtures our eternal focus of faith, we will "discard the poor lenses of our bodies, and peer through the telescope of truth into the infinite reaches of immortality." (Helen Keller).

The faithful keep their faces oriented toward the light, so the shadows will always be behind them. They may not even be aware of the encroaching darkness.

With faith,
we are more
honest, true, chaste,
benevolent, and virtuous.
Our regard for others is more
charitable, and our hope is
more comprehensive.

Our
faith has
no temporal,
spatial, or even
spiritual boundary.
It can be experienced
at one and the same time
in the past, the present,
and the future; now
and forever.

Blessed
are those
who apprehend
that our greatest
battles are fought
within the silent
chambers of
our souls.

"Read yourself full, think yourself straight, pray yourself hot, and let yourself go!" (J. Douglas Gibb). The first three admonitions involve faithful preparation and set the stage for purposeful action, when we can really "let ourselves go."

When cultural
collapse is imminent,
external controls are often
imposed to manipulate behavior,
to maintain at least a semblance
of societal steadiness. Our escalating
dependence on laws to regulate moral
discipline says something about us,
and about our critical need for
faith in the infinite wisdom
of our Heavenly Father.

Blessed
are those
who have the
faith to recognize
that life is hard by
the yard, but it is
a cinch by the
inch.

"Seeing the multitudes, he went up into a mountain, and when he was set, his disciples came unto him, and he opened his mouth, and taught them" the be-happy-attitudes that are the bonus blessings of faith. (Matthew 5:1-2).

There
is order
in The Plan
of Salvation,
wherein faithful
obedience has been
established by God
as a principle that
is anchored in
the eternities.

Faith
not only
liberates us
from guilt and
sin, but it also frees
us from incarceration
to confusion, hesitation,
doubt, ignorance, mistrust,
skepticism, suspicion,
uncertainty, and
worry.

All around us,
we see the fulfillment
of the prophecy that we are
living in the Last Days, when the
hearts of men shall fail them, as
their shields of faith begin to falter.
When that happens, Satan rages in their
hearts and stirs them up to anger
against that which is good. He
pacifies others, and lulls
them away into a false
sense of carnal
security.

Blessed
are they who
realize that, as
long as colored
seed catalogs are
printed, faith will
never die.

Faith
involves the
consistent exercise
of moral discipline, that
eternal principles might be
clothed in a more enduring
substance that is not often
easily or conveniently
demonstrated.

Truly did Paul declare, "God hath not given us the spirit of fear, but of power, and of love, and of a sound mind." (2 Timothy 1:7). Faith is clothed best when it is adorned with the power that stems from a courageous heart.

Faith
liberates us
to enjoy peace
of conscience, to
receive the blessings
of the priesthood, to serve
others in more powerful and
significant ways, to resolutely work
toward our potential, to commune
with the Infinite, and to benefit
from all of the other blessings
of The Plan of Salvation as
we move forward into
the eternities.

Blessed
are those
who apprehend
that our greatest
battles are fought
within the silent
chambers of
our souls.

Faith encourages us to "try the virtue of the word of God." (Alma 31:5) We do so, that we might reap its rewards, and with diligence, patience, and long-suffering, harvest the fruit of the Tree of Life from its low hanging branches.

Our
faith
invites us
to enjoy the
influence of the
Holy Ghost, Who, as
a creative consultant,
always stands ready to
offer His constructive
comments relating
to our developing
storyboard.

Faith moves us
beyond dependence
and independence, to a
stimulating interdependent
relationship with Heavenly
Father, Jesus Christ, and
the Holy Ghost.

In order
to regain
our home
in heaven,
we must be
able to rally
faith as little
children
do.

With faith,
we are caught
up in a rapture
where we can almost
hear legions of angels
who confirm that the earth
has become "a machine for
the making of gods."
(Henri Bergson).

Those who
enjoy the fruits
of faith, consecrate
their lives to the Savior,
and throw themselves upon
His altar of sacrifice, whose
foundation is buttressed
by a supernal display
of divine direction
by God the
Father.

If we desire the gift of faith, we must "let go and let God." Only then, will we catch a religious fever that spikes the temperature of our testimonies, and gets our juices flowing.

As our circle of
knowledge expands,
so do the borders of
darkness. The more we
know, the more we need
to learn. It should do no
violence to our faith if we
realize that, with a greater
understanding of doctrinal
truth, there might yet be
additional questions,
even mysteries of
kingdom, that
we wish to
ponder.

It is our
faith that purifies us
from caustic influences,
and decontaminates us from
the toxicity that is so prevalent
in the world. It neutralizes the
homogenization process that
occurs as we are tossed to
and fro by the vagaries
of life.

The day we became members of the Restored Church was the first day of the rest of our lives.

When
situational
ethics guide our
behavior, and when
every man walketh in
his own way, and after
the image of his own god,
the erosion of faith followed
by the chaotic crash of cultural
cohesion and stability is inevitable.

Faith
is based
on neither
ability, nor
inability, but
it does demand
availability.

As we
travel in
faith thru the
harsh wasteland
of Idumea, oases
will spring up in the
desert of life, to slake
our thirst with living water.
Our roots will have become
anchored within bedrock;
even in the law of
the Lord.

The faithful have learned that darkness cannot be carried into a lighted chamber. They seize every opportunity to be enveloped in light. They have learned to face the sunshine, so that the shadows will always be behind them. Darkness will still exist, but its companions that take the form of apprehension, trepidation, uncertainty, and fear will be out of sight and out of mind.

We take a calculated risk
by exposing our vulnerability
when we have been courageously
faithful, but we are confident
that the best way to destroy
our enemies is by making
friends out of
them.

Loyal
professors
of saving faith
are persevering and
they stay focused on the
tasks at hand. Committed
professors begin with the
end in mind and will
only settle for more,
and not less.

If the testimony of Jesus is the spirit of prophecy, then every self-effacing professor of faith becomes a facilitator who helps to bring others of God's children to the knowledge of His Plan; to their own independent testimony of the Savior, and to faith in His Atonement.

We may choose
to endure without
the comfort of faith,
but if we do so, we also
must accept the inevitable
negative consequences that
are tied to unresolved sin.
This makes our endurance
much more painful than
it would otherwise
have needed
to be.

Those who
are blessed with
the humility of faith
regard God, Who knows
everything there is to know
and dwells in heaven from
everlasting to everlasting,
in a reverential awe.

Faith
grounds us,
not on telestial
turf, but on celestial
boulevards that are
paved with gold.

The spiritual sixth sense with which we are blessed may just be the lowest common denominator in the theory of everything. It is our faith that is the grand unifying principle, and although it is indisputable, it nevertheless challenges explanation on a chalkboard.

Only by exercising perfect faith to see all the way to heaven do we understand the creations of God and truly sense His glory.

As we
ascend
the ladder
of faith, rung
by rung, we will
see lightnings and
mountains smoking,
and hear loud thunder
and the voice of trumpets
that speak in a language
that is inarticulate and
yet irrefutable.

Is it easier
to be wicked, and
harder to be righteous?
Is it easier to be sad, and
harder to be happy? Is it easier
to just put your life on cruise
control, and harder to take
the more challenging
and higher road
of faith?

Only if we
incorporate into
our lives the principle
of the unwavering center
of faith, can we recognize
address, reverse, and erase
for once and for all, the
imbalance in our lives.

Faith becomes a celestial bridge that transports the righteous past the vicissitudes of life all the way to the steadiness of the kingdom of God that lies above the turmoil of confusion.

We may be
as scarecrows who
need a brain, tin men
who desperately want a
heart, or cowardly lions
who, more than anything,
need courage, but when
we reach Oz, we will
warm our hands at
the fire of faith.

Jesus
encouraged
us to give ourselves
completely and without
reservation, that we might
enjoy a state of harmony with
Him and synchronization with the
eternities. He asked us to search
without ceasing, that we might
discover within His nature
the divine center of
our faith.

Our faith provides balance in a world that has become befuddled by weights and measures that have been contaminated by the evidence tampering of the adversary.

The level
of our faith
must be elevated
to something more
dynamic than a simple
mechanical observance
of a multiplicity of
ceremonial rules.

Sooner or later,
there is for each of
us who has undergone a
spiritual heart transplant a
moment in the sun, when the
steady light of understanding
illuminates our minds so that
the divine potential of the new
organs audibly beating in our
chests might be confirmed
by a deep and abiding
faith in Christ.

Joseph's coat
of many colors
is a symbol of our
faith that every cloud
has a silver lining and
that even the darkest
night is followed by
a promise at the
dawning of a
new day.

The
attention
and adoration
of the world is a
satanic seduction to
influence us to abandon
our faith and leave our
coats of many colors
hanging unattended
and unused in the
backs of our
closets.

Secular humanism
and other ideologies
that extoll the virtues of the
intellect and demand tangible
proof destroy faith. They divert
us from following a Plan whose
successful execution hinges
upon nourishing the seeds
of innocent faith in a
higher power.

Every discussion of faith must distinguish it from its caricatures. It is not naiveté or gullibility, nor is it wishful thinking. It is more than confidence and greater than optimism. Faith and positive thinking go hand in hand, but faith is far more than just an attitude.

The choice
that was made
by Adam and Eve in
the Garden to choose
the harder right instead of
the easier wrong, obviated the
'Progression Paradox' that had
faced them, wherein they would
have remained forever in "a state
of innocence, having no joy, for
they knew no misery; doing no
good, for they knew no sin."
(2 Nephi 2:23).

Faith
helps us
to cleave
unto honesty,
truth, chastity,
benevolence, and
virtue; thus, to
treat others
kindly.

Focused faith pushes us beyond our normal capacity and instills within us a quiet resolve to lengthen our stride.

The celestial compass of Gospel principles is calibrated to be oriented toward truth, and is always available to guide the faithful to a safe haven. It is also there for those who have lost their way, to bring them into the fold of the Good Shepherd, or to show them how to return to the security of the community of Christ from which they have strayed.

Faith
provides us
with the regularly
recurring reassurance
of a religious recalibration
that autocorrects with
fortuitous frequency
and celestial
precision.

Heavenly
messengers are
as nursemaids to the
nations. They minister by
the power of faith. They use
its resources to reach out and
lift up the downtrodden and
those who are poor in spirit,
wherever and whenever
they may be found.

If we
have unknowingly
taken poetic license with
the foundation principles of
The Plan, or if we have added
needless ecclesiastical embroidery
to Gospel truths, we diminish our
faith to believe, and we must
speedily repent and change
the approach to our
study.

Joseph's coat was a gift from his father, just as we receive the fabric of faith from our Father in Heaven. We can be sure that He has wisely selected every bolt of cloth and has thoughtfully cut each of them to accommodate the pattern He has planned for our lives.

Our testimony
of the truth includes
three essential elements.
At first, we are introduced to
an eternal principle. Second, is our
correct understanding of the Lord's
counsel concerning the principle,
and finally, is our experience
with the principle, which is
the fruits of faith. (See
Galatians 5:2).

There is no revelation where there is no student, and as long as we ask the wrong questions, we will be at odds with faith. Our rational minds will never be able to bridge the gap between the secular and the divine.

At first, it may
be the easier wrong
that appears to be more
convenient, but that is only
because it harmonizes with the
values of Babylon. Worldliness is
all around us, and without the
stabilizing influence of faith
to choose the harder right,
moral equivocation can
far too easily become
the easier way out,
and become the
pattern of our
conduct.

The world
is at a loss for
diagnosis, even as our
faith in the Gospel of Jesus
Christ provides a virtual war chest
of therapies for cold, stony, and hard
hearts, with the Atonement of Jesus
Christ the remedy of choice
for reconciliation.

Faithful
Latter-day
Saints receive
no stipend and no
annuity that could be
linked to participation
in The Plan of Salvation,
but they are provided with
the tools of the trade, that by
the sweat of their brow they might
earn enough to obtain their own
accommodations, pay their bills
on time, and even occasionally
indulge themselves with some
of the finer things of life.
After all, our happiness is
the object and design
of our existence.

We will find ourselves on the path that leads to celestial glory if we accept inspired direction with dedicated purpose. Our discipleship is actively linked to faithful consistency.

Is it easier to be immoral, and more difficult to be virtuous? Is it easier to be slothful, and harder to be upright? Is it the easier way out to be swayed by secular humanism, and harder to be faithful to eternally valid principles?

We lose
our focus and
our faith gradually,
just as we lose the acuity
of our vision over time. Whether
it is the letter of the law or an eye
chart that is beyond our comprehension,
we become legally blind. Having eyes,
we cannot see what is clearly
before our face.

With focused faith, we trust in our instincts to lead us to the highlands of the morning.

Faith makes
it easier to have
lips that have learned
to articulate only positive
expressions of speech and that
never speak guile, and shoulders
that have developed the strength
to bear the burdens of those who
have been battered and bruised
by the vicissitudes of life and
who may be faltering under
the heavy weight of sorrow
or unresolved sin.

We must
venture forth
out of the shadows,
relying upon the guidance
that we receive from the Light
of Christ and the ministering of
angels, if we want to experience
the special familiarity that the
faithful enjoy with the Lord
of all the earth.

All of us
need to muster
the faith to utilize
the divinely designed
accouterments of the multi-
talented Son of Joseph, Who was
the Carpenter of Nazareth. He will
help us construct the stages upon
which we will enact the magnum
opus that is nothing short of
the drama of our lives.

Experience
is the active
ingredient in a
fertile matrix that
was carefully created
by our Father in Heaven
during His preparation of
the petri dish that has been
personalized to match our
individual circumstances,
in the exciting learning
laboratory of life.

Because it
is easy to talk
about our faith in
timid or shallow ways by
retreating into insipid and
colorless verbiage as an easy
way out, we take care that we
do not steer a course away
from the Savior by any
offhand, dismissive,
or inconsiderate,
expressions.

As we rehearse in our minds the expression of our witness that Jesus is our Savior, it is with our faith that we hear the music of a celestial symphony that has been scored for every imaginable instrument. We have the faith to believe that our voice will be heard.

It is
our faith
that charges
our vision with
infinite perspective,
where we experience the
pulsing stream of insight,
intuition, inspiration, and
revelation whose mighty
flow has no spatial
and no temporal
boundary.

If we thoughtlessly postpone our quest for the holy grail of saving faith until we have become spiritually blinded to the Light of Christ, we become subject to the spirit of the devil. When he captures our hearts, they are mutated to become stony and cold, and we lose the capacity to distinguish good from evil and light from darkness. When we exchange the sunshine that is generated by the foundation of faith for wintry weather and worldliness, the Spirit of the Lord will withdraw to visit warmer climes, allowing Satan's icy breath to be sucked into the vortex we have created for him.

From
the Book
of Genesis, the
example of Joseph
teaches us that we all
may enjoy the protection
that is afforded by the
special clothing that
complements, as an
ensemble, our own
coat of many
colors.

At the Bar of Justice, the evidence will be presented, and our previous conformity with or rejection of eternal law will determine our reward or punishment. Our innate capacity to generate faith, with the impetus coming from the Light of Christ, makes the trials of mortality eminently fair. In fact, the deck has been stacked in our favor.

Those with
the faith to choose
the harder right are like
"brave Horatius, the Captain
of the Gate," who declared: "To
each of us upon this earth, death
cometh soon or late. And how can
we die better, than facing fearful
odds, for the ashes of our fathers
and the temples of our gods?"
(Thomas Macaulay).

Faithless souls
see things as they
are, and wonder "Why?"
The focused faithful dream
things that never were, and ask
"Why not?" They work through
their problems, instead of
working around them.

Weakness is a
part of the tapestry that
has been woven by God into
the fabric of our lives. We simply
turn to the inventory of thread that
He has provided for us, that enables us
to weave colorful new patterns that
are a more accurate expression of
the celebration of our faith in
the Atonement of Christ.

The
light of the
Spirit gives every
thread in the fabric of
our own faith a vitality,
vim, vigor, and vivacity that
is unique to holy vestments.
Their steadfast colors will
never fade, save it be thru
neglect or unbelief. They
will remain impervious
to blemishes, but for
the stubborn stains
of unresolved
sin.

Faith
encourages us to
constantly strive to
do more, to be better, to
seek understanding, and to
empower ourselves with wisdom.
We emulate the Olympic motto:
"Citius, Altius, Fortius," or
"Faster, Higher, Stronger.

The
Holy Ghost
stimulates soul-sweat
as He works on our sense
of duty, our conscience,
and our scruples, to
slowly nurture our
faith to believe.

Faith is the
great equalizer,
no matter in what
exclusive ecclesiastical
country club we may hold
a membership, or upon what
narrow theological terrace
we may have paused to
catch our breath.

Those with the faith to choose the harder right, instead of the easier wrong, view their afflictions, their trials and their tribulations, in a new light, and determine to discover how they can work to their benefit.

How can we muster the faith to keep the commandments? Our Father has revealed the key: "Repent ye, and be baptized in the name of my Beloved Son." (2 Nephi 31:11).

Faith makes it
easier to have backs
that have become sturdy
enough to brace us against
the fierce winds of adversity
and the wiles of the adversary,
and hearts that are receptacles
of pure and virtuous principles
upon which we may draw
in times of need.

Far too many
of us, by seeking the
approbation of the world,
allow ourselves to be tossed
about as flotsam and jetsam
on the sea of life, never to
enjoy the sweet blessing
of spiritual centricity
that can flow out
of faith.

It is the shield of faith that protects us from all of the worldly contaminants of our material prosperity, as well as from the temptation to fill space with telestial trinkets that can canker our souls if they are viewed or used unwisely.

Our faith
sustains us as
we receive with
equanimity whatever
comes our way during
the incubation period of
our spiritual metamorphosis
that was designed to be just
as challenging as it would
be rewarding.

Innumerable
gurus have guided
our lives with a profound
influence that has helped us
to nurture the tender feelings
that have shaped our
faith to believe.

The supernal gift of faith is catalyzed by an infusion of the heavenly element.

The faith
with which we have
been blessed surprises us in
myriad and delightful ways. It
cultivates a culture of reflection,
keeps the Savior in our thoughts,
nurtures an eternal perspective,
initiates positive change, and
harmonizes our behavior
with His charitable
example.

We persevere
in faith because
we do not want to
be spiritually starved,
doctrinally dehydrated,
or intellectually inhibited
while only inches away from
the living bread that could
have satisfied our hunger,
or from the fountains of
living water that could
have slaked our thirst
or even healed us of
our sins or our
blemishes.

Our faith
envelops us
in a shower of
divinely directed
diamond dust that
glitters with thousands
of points of light and
reflections from
above.

Blessed are they who, when they at first don't succeed, realize they are about average. The difference between those who are failures and those who are winners, is that the winners have the faith to try just one more time than they fail.

Faith
unshackles us
from the unpleasant
consequences of Justice.
Darkness is the conjoined twin
of misery, but the obedience of faith
frees us to embrace the truth, to make
intelligent choices, to perform purposefully,
to carry on convincingly, and to progress
persistently; in short, to rise above the
cares of the world through the
Atonement of Christ.

There
is order
in The Plan
of Salvation,
wherein faithful
obedience has been
established by God
as a principle that
is anchored in
its bedrock.

It
is by
faith that
we are able
to envision the
happiest place on
earth. We realize that
it is only if we return to
our psychological, spiritual,
and emotional childhood that
we may rediscover the place
where dreams really
do come true.

When a faithless society is weighed in the balances and is found wanting, it can all be traced to their spiritually bankruptcy on an institutional scale.

Obstacles are those frightful things we see when we take our minds off our goals. They loom large with gratuitous significance. Our faith endows us with the vision to see beyond these potential stumbling blocks. It empowers us to rely upon the expansive, creative engine for positive change that is the Gospel, by turning them into stepping-stones that pave the way to higher achievement.

With faith,
we are more
trusting and we
speak without guile.
We are more transparent
and less prejudicial. We have
fewer pretensions and are more
genuine. We are less prone to
make excuses and quicker
to seek the forgiveness
of the Lord, as well as
to forgive others.

Always looking
for the easy way out
condemns us to negotiate
the instability of shaky ground,
as opposed to the solid footing that
Gospel sod affords to those whose
actions are consistent with the
courage of faith.

The faithful know how to turn stumbling blocks into stepping stones. Crisis becomes opportunity, and victory is snatched from the jaws of defeat. They know that "change comes like a flash of lightning and a clap of thunder. The people shrink in fear, but after the storm, flowers bloom." ("I Ching").

Because
of the courage
of our faith, we will
never thirst, because our
taproots have pushed down
thru Gospel topsoil until they
have reached a free, full,
flowing fountain of
living water.

Faith probes us for pliability. It searches us for submissiveness, and it measures us for meekness. These hone our humility even as they elevate us to higher states of energy.

Courage blesses
us with an abundance
of faith, even the faith to
take risks. We break free from
the safety nets, the comfort zones,
and the ports of refuge to which the
timid apprehensively retreat at the
first sign of danger, to squeak
out their lives as they scurry
about from one shadowy
sanctuary to another
in a flight from
faith.

The faithful know the face of fear, but they look beyond it, to an "enchanted wood where the foliage is always green, where joy abides, and where nightingales nest and sing, and where life and death are one in the presence of the Lord Jesus." (Helen Keller).

As we faithfully carry out our work, and quietly face our obligations, the righteousness of our cause will be revealed in marvelous simplicity and in plainness. Walls of opposition to our progress will crumble and fall away as the Savior comforts us and succors us with the bread of life.

We must
have the courage
of faith if we hope to
be able to successfully face
the demons which play a role in
the opposition in all things that has
been built into our experiences. In
the fight or flight scenario, faith
becomes the launch pad for the
anticipated adrenalin rush
that carries us beyond
our night terrors.

Faithful professors who are dedicated to discipline are not prone to distraction, nor are they likely to be easily persuaded, while imaginative professors of faith are creative and even prophetic.

Those who are physically past their prime can still faithfully endure to the end. It may be of some consolation to realize that when we are over the hill, we really do pick up speed.

Real professors of faith hunger and thirst after righteousness, and they are filled with the Holy Ghost. They press forward with dedication, feasting on the scriptures. They receive physical and spiritual nourishment, and they endure to the end with continuing responsibility and accountability.

God
allows us
to be tested and
tempted so that we
can show ourselves and
all the heavens if we have
the faith that is necessary
for us to go the second
mile; to see what our
spiritually aerobic
fitness level
really
is.

When we have
the faith to go
the second mile,
our obedience is no
longer inconvenient,
and we experience the
soul-expanding desire
to more unreservedly
labor in the traces
beside the Lord
our God.

Those who have been
blessed with the nobility of
faith have somehow been able to
break free of "the influence of that
spirit which hath so strongly riveted
the creeds of the fathers, who have
inherited lies, upon the hearts of
the children, and filled the
world with confusion.
(D&C 123:7).

Faith leaves its distinct afterglow from our premortal lives that establishes a subtle link between the heavens and the earth that is undeniable.

The Hubble telescope can "see" 13.2 billion light years into our past, almost back to the moment of creation itself, but it cannot gaze into heaven for five minutes.

Some explain
our connection by
faith with the eternities
as déjà vu, from the French,
literally meaning "already seen,"
in order to emotionally embrace
and explain the phenomenon of
having the strong sensation that
a current event has already
been experienced.

The light
of the body
is the eye, and
when it is single
to the faith to see
into heaven above,
our elements below
will be stirred by
its warm glow,
as we become
captivated by
the Spirit.

Faith molds
us in mortality,
and establishes us
in eternity. We learn
to respond to heavenly
smiles, so that one day,
we might become engaged
as performers in celestial
symphonies.

Disorder
and progression
must ultimately be
in balance with each
other. In fact, it was
ordained in heaven that
there must be a healthy
juxtaposition of opposing
forces for faith to prevail
as the first principle in
revealed religion.

If we
ignore the
celestial laws
that are the only
homing beacons that
are powerful enough to
penetrate the swirling mists
of darkness in our telestial
world, we have tacitly chosen
an alternative course leading
to our destruction, as we run
aground on the rocky coasts
of faithlessness.

With
spiritual
sensitivity and
the preparation of
faith, we find that the
time for action has
arrived.

Faith blesses us
with the knowledge
that mortality is only
a tiny fraction of a much
larger reality, and that our
perspective is faulty only
when we believe it
to be unique.

In the beginning,
it was the Gods who
organized and gave form
to the heavens and the earth
by demarcating the boundaries
of the temporal universe, not to
mention the eternal worlds. (See
Abraham 4:1). It was thru faith
that they created all things,
and defined existence
itself.

Our faith
blesses us to move
about freely, but it is
always available to guide
us to the path of safely, to
find shelter within the sphere
of God's protective influence,
where we may be shielded from
lethal storms whose suffocating
tempests of devious doctrine
threaten to suck the life-
sustaining marrow from
our bones.

Professors of faith recognize the positive and pleasant aspects of endurance. Faith carries a performance requisite that motivates them to maintain spiritually aerobic fitness, that they might meet the unwavering demands of their discipleship without fatiguing their faith.

We retain the purity of our faith, when it has convicted us of our sins and we have turned to the Savior with full purpose of heart.

Faith welcomes
the trials we face, and
views them as nothing but
pop quizzes in the learning
laboratory of life. They prepare
us for the final exam that will
come at the conclusion of
our mortal curriculum.

Sooner or later,
every member of the
Church is ordained to
become a faithful second
miler who is admonished to
run, and not just walk, to the
end of their lives, as they seek
new ways to build the Church
and Kingdom of God
on the earth.

As long as we remain trapped in time, we can only indirectly appreciate the eternities.

Faith prepares us
to move onward along
a steady course of progress
without encumbering ourselves
with the wobbly constraints of
uncertainty that always lie in
wait to mislead those who
manifest a timid and
hesitant spiritual
constitution.

Allowing
Gospel principles to
release us from captivity
through faith permits us to
see things as they really are,
and to enjoy a lucidity that
comes more from the heart
than from the head.

The formula
that defines the
equations of the divine
center of faith is at the very
heart of the eternal laws that
have power to carry us beyond
the conventional boundaries
of our every day world.

The gate
may be strait,
and the way narrow,
but those who accept Christ
as their Guide will find that it
is within their capacity to travel a
path of progression by threading the
eye of the needle and walking a fine
line past the seemingly unalterable,
unavoidable, and unstoppable
demands of disproportion.

For faith to prevail, opposition must exist as the basis of a matrix of mayhem, within which the fiery darts of the adversary trace an incendiary trail of disorder.

It is by our
faith to see all
the way to heaven
that the power of the
Holy Ghost is released
to penetrate the barriers
that isolate us from the
sum and substance of
our existence that
more accurately
define reality.

Those who have been card carrying members of The Church of Jesus Christ long enough to have experienced a liberal measure of temporal, spiritual, emotional, and intellectual symmetry, may sometimes ask our Heavenly Father why His Spirit allows the world to tug at them? Why is it that their faith in Christ is not yet perfect?

Because of our faith, we willingly surrender our agency to Christ, knowing that it is a necessary and vital step on our path of progress that leads to eternal life.

Deferential professors are faithful, and they endure, that they might obtain the prize of eternal life. They claim the promises of the Lord, Who said He would disperse the powers of darkness from before them, and would cause the heavens to shake for their good.

Unassuming
professors of faith
are light bearers who
carry the torch of truth
as a beacon to guide those
who are having difficulty finding
their way home. The best among them
wear the heavy robes of responsibility
of God's priesthood, or operate
under its influence and
at its direction.

Inventive professors build the foundation of their faith on bedrock, and they have depth and breadth. Inspired professors make regular deposits to their spiritual bank accounts, from which they are free to take timely and strategic withdrawals.

Some recognize the anchor of faith as intuition, or as the capacity to understand something without the need for our conscious reasoning. It is in good company, for it draws upon insight, and is the precursor of not only inspiration, but also revelation.

For the faithful, both the heavens and the earth are bathed in celestial fire that is akin to background radiation that still lingers from the cataclysmic moment of creation itself.

Our faith teaches us that we are God's chosen people, and that we live within His embrace, enjoying a security that others do not know.

About The Author

Phil Hudson and his wife Jan have 7 children and over 25 grandchildren. They enjoy spending time with their family at their cabin nestled in the Selkirk Mountains, on the shore of Priest Lake, the crown jewel of North Idaho. Phil had a successful dental practice in Spokane, Washington for 43 years, before retiring in 2015. He has an eclectic mix of hobbies, and enjoys the out of doors. He always finds time, however, to record his thoughts on his laptop, and understands Isaac Asimov's response when he was asked: If you knew that you had only 10 minutes left to live, what would you do?" He answered: "I'd type faster."

Phil received the inspiration to write this book while he and Jan were serving as missionaries for The Church of Jesus Christ of Latter-day Saints, in the Kingdom of Tonga. While there, they celebrated their 50th wedding anniversary.

Those who
have embraced
the divine center
of faith will follow
the yellow brick road
with their heart, might,
mind, and strength
until they reach
the Emerald
City of
Oz.

By The Author

Essays

- Volume One: Spray From The Ocean Of Thought
- Volume Two: Ripples On A Pond
- Volume Three: Serendipitous Meanderings
- Volume Four: Presents Of Mind
- Volume Five: Mental Floss
- Volume Six: Fitness Training For The Mind And Spirit

First Principles and Ordinances Series

- Faith - Our Hearts Are Changed
- Repentance - A Broken Heart and a Contrite Spirit
- Baptism - One Hundred And One Reasons Why We Are Baptized
- The Holy Ghost - That We Might Have His Spirit To Be With Us
- The Sacrament - This Do In Remembrance Of Me

Book of Mormon Commentary

- Volume One: Born In The Wilderness
- Volume Two: Voices From The Dust
- Volume Three: Journey To Cumorah

Doctrine & Covenants Commentary

    Volume One - Sections 1 - 34
    Volume Two - Sections 35 - 57

Minute Musings: Spontaneous Combustions of Thought

    Volume One
    Volume Two
    Volume Three

Calendars:

    In His Own Words: Discovering William Tyndale
    As I Think About The Savior
    Scriptural Symbols

Children's Books

    Muddy, Muddy
    The Thirteen Articles of Faith
    Happy Birthday

Doctrinal Themes

    The House of the Lord

A Thought For Each Day of the Year

    Faith
    Repentance
    Baptish
    The Holy Ghost
    The Sacrament
    The House Of The Lord
    The Atonement
    The Plan Of Salvation

Professional Publications

    Diode Laser Soft Tissue Surgery Volume One
    Diode Laser Soft Tissue Surgery Volume Two
    Diode Laser Soft Tissue Surgery Volume Three

These, and other titles, are available from online retailers.

Disorder
roughly takes
us further from the
influence of the Spirit,
whose purpose is to guide
us away from the precipice of
destruction, and to lead us to
that secure sanctuary where
the stability of higher
laws abides.

Quid magis possum dicere?

www.ingramcontent.com/pod-product-compliance
Lightning Source LLC
Chambersburg PA
CBHW060507240426
43661CB00007B/948